Shepherd's Warning, Shepherd's Delight

Shepherd's Warning, Shepherd's Delight

Patrick McLuskie

EDITING ASSISTANCE BY
Liesl Johnstone

RESOURCE *Publications* • Eugene, Oregon

SHEPHERD'S WARNING, SHEPHERD'S DELIGHT

Copyright © 2020 Patrick McLuskie. All rights reserved. Except for brief quotations in critical publications or reviews, no part of this book may be reproduced in any manner without prior written permission from the publisher. Write: Permissions, Wipf and Stock Publishers, 199 W. 8th Ave., Suite 3, Eugene, OR 97401.

Resource Publications
An Imprint of Wipf and Stock Publishers
199 W. 8th Ave., Suite 3
Eugene, OR 97401

www.wipfandstock.com

PAPERBACK ISBN: 978-1-7252-5490-9
HARDCOVER ISBN: 978-1-7252-5491-6
EBOOK ISBN: 978-1-7252-5492-3

Manufactured in the U.S.A.   04/08/20

To the memory of my father,
who learnt of this book
in our last conversation
together in this world.

With sincere thanks to Jana,
who would not give up praying for me.

But He replied to them, "When it is evening, you say, 'It will be fair weather, for the sky is red.' And in the morning, 'There will be a storm today, for the sky is red and threatening.' Do you know how to discern the appearance of the sky, but cannot discern the signs of the times?"

—Jesus, Matt 16:2–3 (NASB)

A Place of Belonging

Two rivers flow;
they reach around
plains that set
their toil down,
beneath the cloud-form
whited peaks
a city bows
deep to the east.
It is the land Ngāi Tahu bore;
Ōtautahi, the land; our
settlers saw
and lent to it
another name,
two parents now;
in Christ became.

Patrick McLuskie
Aotearoa New Zealand.

Contents

Preface | xi

His Poor Materials | 1
Night | 3
Dawn | 33
Light | 65

Look, Here Comes That Fool | 91

About the Author | 181

Preface

Shepherd's Warning, Shepherd's Delight is a poetic description of my walk from a lost place, to a place of relationship with God. Raised Catholic, I wandered away from organized Christian faith and became more interested in an abstract connection with a Creator, through Eastern belief and healing systems. While *Shepherd's Warning, Shepherd's Delight* doesn't directly address these systems, it does give voice to the underlying soul-call that cries out for and seeks a personal relationship with the Living God. Darkness becomes light, becomes life. But the pathways aren't smooth or idealized. The journey oscillates and there is always the underlying realization of one's humanity; the very real and flawed part of us that is in such need of a Savior.

Shepherd's Warning, Shepherd's Delight ultimately takes on observations of the state of the world and the churches. It assumes that the found faith is rooted in the belief that the Bible is what it claims to be; simply, God's Word given to us. Hence the title; the Bible as the foundation of our knowledge of faith is both our supreme delight and our greatest test. We are indeed all being warned.

His Poor Materials

"By the sweat of your face
You will eat bread,
Till you return to the ground,
Because from it you were taken;
For you are dust,
And to dust you shall return."

—The Lord God, Gen 3:19 (NASB)

I
NIGHT

winter solstice

some winters are longer than the season
as they link their arms and will not budge,
so friends try to force a little
springtime between them,
these winters of your soul; you pass the times
by a fire without warmth and you dream
of days to come, when laughter will once again
bubble like spring in your step,

and you blame the wind
and you blame the snow,
and you blame the thunder
but you know that which has always been;
the winter is yours alone, and alone you will remain

tormented time

tormented time abounds
in the sweet new light;
this day unfolding
as the morning paper
crisp and clean,
for sectional dissection
of trivial minutiae,
as boy bludgeons man
and country would country
upon misery is piled,

by the back door,
for the rubbish man
to remove out of sight,
into the ground,
and maybe a fossil of fuel
in seventy million years or less,
for some combustion of which type
I can less imagine
than the recycled reality
of daily time,
in the torment of now.

Mockingbird

Mock me
say the mocking bird;
Mock the one
who thought he heard,
a voice, a call
from heaven above,
a light, a bird shaped like a dove,
that drove its beak
right through my heart,
so hope and care
did then depart,
from this place
of limpid dreams,
left this place of empty screams,
to moonlit sky
above my head,
I am alone,
my careless dread.

the faithful mutt

the faithful mutt
lies on the sand
the sky it beckons
the master's hand
was laid upon
his faithful life
he felt the strings
the faithful wife,
who looked each time
the rocking chairs
back and forth
the empty fears,
there is no one
up in the sky
there is no He
who rocks He lies—
the sand it burns
his faithful back
the chair it taunts
his mongrel's lack
of knowing of
His hidden ways
of finding in
our rocking days

little friends

my friend he stalks me
day by day
in other ways
I'm made to lie
down 'fore the pillars
of the hour
that call the sky
my vaunted stars,
to the earth of salt and grist
upon its mortar is ground the list
of such beauty true and fair
and ashes scattered
in the air,
to blow up to the lucid sun
who burns my hopes
my homeward run,
and as he trips me
by the line
that tangles round
my neck in time,
to see the substance
drained from me
and with it all formality,
no tie, no coat
upon my back
the paternal cord
His sceptre hacks,
and leaves me to
my little friend
who likes it when
my soul depends
upon his beaming promises
and in the end
his lowly bed

The Bottle

I should very much like to be that ship
in the bottle.
Polished wood and brass gleam resplendently,
shielded from the corrosive salt of doubt.

Minute perfection in detail absorbed, a scale replica of the
Son's memory.
Rigging threaded sublime, sails engorged, cork secure,
all safe from sin's gravitational pull.

How did it come to be so?
What trick of the Mariner's calloused hand?
What age-long secret whispered, did erect that
which could not fit?

For I,
caught in the boiling sea. The reef's jagged smile beckoning.
Mast tall and unbowed,
yet sails lacerated, rigging like some wild vine.

I,
who would oppose the walk of the tides.
Who cannot fit but to break into
pieces.

What fate, what faith to have
that trick?
What far shore now beckons
on the eternal horizon of despair?

The Well

I pray the dark prayer
of the damned,
from deep within this well
the light of the earth,
a dew drop on high,
sparking with promise,
a glint of grace
in the hole
into which my soul crawled,
like a many-legged beast
of exoskeleton,
and inside the soft corruption
of a promise never fulfilled,
the warm voice of will,
vice-like friend,
Until I fell
into darkness
did my pride feel the way,
and that drop,
that sweet dew drop
of grace
is all I have,
a silk thread of light,
a silk thread of life;
till the cool voice of Eve,
her mark upon my soul,
my hope
and my companion calls.

Are You There?

In the quiet moments,
a fraud
is set upon me.
This; my share of three times deity,
is not assured by the time
and this place of my abode;
Instead loneliness and longing;
I hear the distant calling.

Do I seek and cannot find
that rest and self-creation
lost in eternal time?
His life a crossing of two lines.
It too was of the flesh
in which I pace
gazing on,
through the bars of mortal iron.

Can we seek
but not to see?
Is the frozen pond upon the wall
about to fall, and fall?
And then what chance
to solve the puzzle
of those splinters in the ground,
shattered; never found.

That reflection of me,
the God within me please,
thrown upon the stone. . .
In this cage I pace, atone.

Us

The beast with many heads;
I may not ask its name,
as it stalks the dark places
where tears form salt seas
that flow low before
and will not deny...
Who dares to stand
and look in its eye?
As the innocents of time
and a far empty place
call to the night
and it answers with hate—
The beast with many heads;
I may know its name...
It is us.
We are its heads,
as we turn from the light
and cast to the night
where the innocents
are lost in our shame.

On Cold Steps

Oh buildings of stone, cold
is your countenance;
you lay your steps before me
and in welcome
you are gracious,
but within your walls
there is no laughter,
for the children
do not play here;
you chased them away
with high words and canon
that rained upon their youth,
and in their time of flowering
they knew only of your harshness
and of your stone, cold
to their young touch.

The Temple

And the temple stood at the top of the hill
And it proclaimed that through its doors
The faithful could see He who is unseen,
And it granted itself all rights and privileges
Associated with such august promontory
And it was white and it gleamed in the sun,
And the faithful filed through its doors and gave
And the temple grew resplendent in its own eyes,
But the colour on the inside was not right,
And the rules confused the simple
And filled the minds of the truth-seeking souls
Who could no longer see through the walls,
And who were told to stand in line
In order that they could see Him who cannot be seen—
And many great schisms occurred yet the temple stood and it gleamed,
And the second new world peoples gathered at its doors
While the old and new world peoples
Grew tired and walked away.

A True Church Divided

Church divided,
squabbling rooms, look up
see your common roof,
supported
not by the walls that divide
but by the spaces within,
now shout your praise and behold:
One space
One roof
One truth

The Wailing Ones

upon the world
of walking men,
waking men, of scolding men,
came a voice
before the sea
from the north
within the breeze,
nothing good
can come from there;
wise men walked,
woke they scolded,
the life of God
then unfolded,
sandals trod upon
the earth;
dust to dust
the wall was cursed,
and to the breeze
wailing tongues,
told their tales in
lore long sung,
of rebellion,
prophets born,
of roaming life and
endless scorn,
of death in places
behind the wire;
of walls that dwarf the
rocket fire

Piggy-Wig Knew

Blessed be the pig,
snout immersed in the glories
of the trough of life
that he may gorge,
will he fill of this swill,
fine wines and petit fours sloshing
while the husks of luxury chassis
grind together,
as his teeth pulverize
the essential items
of the mail-order list
to the substance of Cain;
Sweet revenge,
as the slop passes through
that which sought it
and never a drop
of life given; run
as it does from the other end,
where at least
it comes to rest
in a sort of peace
in the ground,
from which the pig grew,
into the only life he knew.

blind time

in dimness in darkness
so draw down the blinds
close out the light
through the cracks it still winds,
block it and smother it
and curse it this time
in the absence of light
the blackness as wine,
gulped down in wonderful
silk-woven drops,
it deadens the vessel
yes,
the light does it mock

Lying still and cold

I saw the spark had gone,
I saw that spark of life
had left that small rabbit,
and I didn't understand
what made life
at once, and then gone.

My chemistry set apart;
mute upon the table,
to bake the base elements
and would it come again, that spark,
as I sat and was afraid
of the fabric between the worlds.

The world of life, stillborn death
and the tearing of that curtain
but a flick of fate's switchblade,
and I knew
and could never escape,
the menace of that flick.

Salaration

I call the seconds now, come back,
to he who has let you spring
like sand-hoppers from his picnic rug,
I was with you but not within you.

Precious metals of potential unseen
by a watchful eye; no shutter snap
to say there in this picture, still,
is what I will carry forward for all time—

My memory of you, child,
lest the seconds laugh last and best,
at the man self-crucified
on the salaried cross.

The Leaving

Could a tombstone
be shaped rectangular
and green
and lie down
with its coating atop
for the feet of the gone
here first stepped there,
who rolled
and then kicked
at spheres
then pedalled;
See the tears that were shed
and the games
with the shame
of absent fathers,
whose feet too seldom
felt the cool brush
of a time
when all was one
and then none.

Fallen Shepherd

Witching, whiling
all beguiling,
a snake that moves
entwining, winding.
Within the truth
there sleeps the hidden,
self-seeded doubt;
a miner's midden.
Oh movement deep within
the ground,
magma scoping,
creeping, finding.
Searching for
the light of now;
an eruption here
to blind the host
of the good,
the sanctified;
A death in life
for the deified.

Crystal Sow

Sit there little man;
wrap your eyes around it,
like cellophane
let it absorb you.
Your mouth,
frozen in mid-chew;
You,
child of the crystal sow,
look to suckle
on the milk-flow of poison.
Images you think you understand,
as I,
your loving parent
place you
on the altar of carpet.
That it may take you
and so appease
my mind,
who could not have left
you staring at the wall.
While I gather
around me
the objects of my desire.
That make me
more than
I am
in their eyes,
but less than nothing
to your
faraway stare.

Waiting to Die

Blue rinse hair on sandstone heads, still,
contrasting floral sweeps adorn
ersatz paper clinging to death's waiting room;
behold, aluminium protrusions and action replay conversations
deflected by stony masks as errant neurons run riot,
sniping at memories past the point of return
from this entombment wrought
by well-meaning ones once cradled,
who know "what's best for you dear."
Not ours to say our hearts are asunder,
"but sit with them and wait you to die,"
so we may carve the cake of your dignity soon.

free-falling

of self in free-fall
and descent
upon the stones
of riverbed spent

dry as in
the drought of gain
of dust and faeces
spend the pain

not knowing of
the road arcane
a work of fiction
sends the cane

across the back
of the centred man
and within the stripes
the measured plan

bacon rind

the vultures circle around the thing
lying prone before their king
and were it not for the beast
as the birds disgorge their feast

and eat the flesh of him who wept
at the last dam-burst of promises kept;
the thing he stammered for more time,
now let him shred like bacon rind

sliced upon the butcher's block
the vultures fly and turn the lock
to send the man unto the deep
and dark is the place that the vultures keep

The way of falling

Preening splendid birds;
your bright colours
dazzle those jealous eyes,
high in your tree tops.

But beware,
the roots of those trees
lie shallow across the earth.

Care not, preening birds
for the forest floor;
the carpet of humanity.

Care not for that which rots
and gravity will call;
call you down . . .

Your magnificent canopy
with the falling tree,
it will come,
you will come.

The dank touch of earth's litter
will be your bed,
it will be your bread.

And how will the sun
seek out your back
as the dusk mist
prints your colours grey?

Seek not the light of this world
splendid birds;
care now and repent,
fallen world.

heart-string

thin curtain, thin veil,
creature behind you
whom do you hail?
twice cloven hoof
withering eye,
a piercing blue light
scoop of the sky,
high mounted beast
within the black steed,
on wind you have flown,
spawn of your seed;
the mana you've led
to the dearth of a culture,
leave now with your mark—
the scar of the vulture

the other one

curse the angel who cursed the Son
black broken wings
fallen one,
upon the bench of choice is laid
upon the soul
the price is paid

Undertow, against the flow

Life flows	Life flows	Life flows
I know	I know	I know
I say	I say	I say
I, no	I, no	I know
Life grows	Life grows	Life grows
I know	I, know	I, no
I, care	I care	I do not care
I am bare	I am bare	I am bare
Life shows	Life shows	Life shows
I should	I should	I would
I who would	I who would	I who should
I could	I, could	I could
Life sows,	Life sows,	Life sows,
I stand	I stand	I withstand
I withstand,	I withstand	I understand
I, as quicksand	I as quicksand	I am, quicksand

Denial

weary bones stand alone
before the door
of self-denial

the lock set fast
to the rhythmic beat
of the head against the iron

the blood trickling down
is the price wherein
the keeper's door will open

and upon the brow
the scar stands proud
of the denial of damnation

— II —
DAWN

Prodigal

You will
your will
not mine,
but I lie.

Pack your bags
and run,
shirt sleeves flapping;
chase the setting sun.

Door swinging wide,
safe cocoon forgone,
on the streets
I hide.

His house standing empty
the Lord will place a sentry
keeping watch
for me.

Living a little rough
wallet's nearly empty,
guess I'll return
when I please.

a place

a place,
a simple space
for me to rest

my head,
my body,
my bones apart

from the world,
weary world,
dreary world,

my place
with gold
and the wind

and keen
am I
to walk

the margins
between my place
and the blue beyond,

as it breathes
and it sighs
and it washes away

my weary life

Time Shadows

As I sit with my father
on the rocks of this shore,
as a young boy,
he is here.

His presence magnified
by the void that is half a life time;
a ribbon woven path,
my understanding of time
has curled past this place.

I am here
I am here
I was here

Where the sea laughs
and calls me remember,
whether I wish to
or not.

Faithful feet I have trusted
to carry me on,
my life
my curling ribbon,
may I have my time
again?

The Door

Can it be, that which seems unconquerable
is where all paths lead?
A door, locked,
the key thrown against the abyss
only to return
like some accursed boomerang;
a life-time of twists and curves
to end up here, still.

Feet quiet now and parallel,
hand stretched at rest against the blockade;
what will, what energy
to go back to those shaded paths?
to see one's own footprints on ground too well worn;
a certain waste of life.

To pick it up then and turn the key
is all that need be done,
knowing that but one path
lies just beyond.

Freedom of Sorts

Must I choose from the yokes
placed before me by their chattering promoters?
as marketplace peddlers; "Try this on Sir;
one size fits all for a discount today."

On which field will I plough
happy in the work of the Lord,
back bent by the burden
of a doctrinal cartload of stones?

A peasant of God is no warrior's cast-off;
oh rejoice in the sweet sweat
of the brow, let it drip and drain into the soil;
you could follow it too.

In the lap

As I rest my head
In the lap of hope

It is comfortable here,
I am warm,
I will not leave,

But my body detaches
And walks from my head

To do the things
That bodies do,
While I watch it

Then realize with sadness
That the one needs the other

So I call it over;

I hope it will come to this lap
That could be its home too.

Mid-life Spices

may I take your hand and lead you in a dance
through the door to the right,
the one marked by the sign of the lamb;
a shepherd's corridor so to speak

and on the other side to what
if you will, if your will said I could,
would you join that small dance of hope,
a quickstep of love,

and before the twilight hour
when the low threatening dusk
causes the contemplation
of such things;

rather now
in the full tide of noon,
that the mid-spice reflect
upon a long-shadowed doom

the divine fluid

an insufficient grip
is all I have of you
my dear lost thing,

from the bottom of this well
the consciousness lost
in the currents
as refuge floats
down the mainstream of time;

material life, material strife
how you wash away
the echoes of the voice
I yearn to hear
I need to hear
and must divine
from the desert sands
of this stillborn life,

water deep and clear
the fluid of the gods
spent on the desert bloom,
let it bloom,

let me feel this thirst quenched
lest I throw my cup
to the desert jackals
that they may worship it hence

Shooting Horses

if they shoot horses
will they shoot mine?
winged beast,
riding upon the salient
of heaven,

and would I fall with him?
limp in form,
back to the earth
from whence I came,

my penance
for a soaring countenance,
sprung from the well
of the successes
wrought
on the high anvil;

for me
the soft and malleable iron,

knowing not my place,
till the damp touch
of mortality
cools my white form;
into that which
the divine hammer sought

The book of a life

I live in my illusion,
I live in my delusion
of a steady sort of state
to my story,
as a flick of the pages
will reveal,
linear words march
as cannon fodder
to be enfiladed
on the deathbed
of a chapter
named the last;
the sole book of words
I may lay at the feet
of One who would read
and would judge,
the publication of my voice
in the long halls
of shelves of the eternal kind,
or not.

grave recollections

make it of granite, that cross of mine
let it sit atop me glaring dully
in the cool winter sun

that it may speak to its cousins huddled near,
all looking for something;
something to do, to say

as they cast lots for the birds
that come to rest but will not stay,
and still no conversation from below

for that soul has walked from its dusty seat
through here to there
but not back again;

so alone is the close
as beetles scurry with eyes averted
from this bedroom of mortal toil

but a child with a posy stops to remember,
and laughs and runs and skips
as all adults should

my metronome

I rest upon the cooling stone
a finger floats
metronome,
a tag upon my toe
has pleased
the attention of the throng;
is seized.

As I lie upon the stone
the finger stops
it points alone,
into the direction of the past; to
those in the pit,
my die is cast.

As they lay, adoring feast
upon the table
of the least;
seems the passing
of the time
transformed all memory,
how sublime.

One who sinned, knew the shame
life cut short
forsake the blame,
attach it not
to the near-deceased
let bitter herbs
find their release.

Sanctification of the passed
a revolving door
do angels laugh?
no growth nor graft, the telling kind
a life of me
may God be blind—

Be Empty

Behold the vessel filled with the decay of life
still corner of the garden come,
as passing rain sometimes searches out
a little water gathers with the infill.

And the syrup formed scorns the dark ravens
even that would bathe in form laughing;
for what would I clean it
to empty and to scourge it?
back to the base material of its kind,
smooth conscience to the touch
yet no witness to the eye
in this still hidden corner.

And would the Spirit come
in downpour rain as tears cast,
a monsoon of tension broken
that the life-giver would surge?

And the calm following on
elixir still and clear,
that brilliant reflection, come the rise
of the Eternal Son.

coffin people

can't you see walking coffins
brass eyes dull and cold to the Word?
how a beauty of thin veneer
screens the base wood,

inside which, bones and knuckles roam free,
faux-attractive thing
may these brass eyes ever void
these your hidden sins;

your bones rattle round
white dice dance and conceal,
roll them forth yes, await
what the runes would reveal;

could the throw of the bones
set you free through luck's door?
you so aloft from the yoke dangling there
a noose as it were sent to strangle your fall,

but this death you denied
was the truth and the life,
the way your heart knew
but still you fled,

to the left all along and was it so done,
would your brass eyes reflect
the truth
that you're dead

The Coming

Your life, you
facade-like beings,
can I walk
through this western
movie town,
you smiling at me
from each side,
flower pot jewellery
adorns your pretty faces,
the showdown
that goes on
on the street
that you see
is the struggle
of death with life,
and you look
and you smile,
high-noon marks
the time
the hour
you know not the time,
it could be upon you
now,
and how
would you stand
if I were to peek
behind the facade
and see
the set-maker's props,
holding you there,
the body of your dwelling
empty and bare,
would you smile
if the sheriff was in town,
can you find
your deputy's badge
now?

Conformer

And when did you, reformer,
become the keeper of the safe,
when did that thirst for truth
become quenched by the liquid of success?

What cosy hearth now awaits,
shutters tight to the hammering winds of doubt,
recollections filling the present,
the present is the past?

And what of the future,
what chalice now passed to those
whose minds grow impatient,
asking all that may be asked?

And what of you, reformer,
has the journeyman's road been too long,
was the answer ever around this bend,
or does the draught of the eternal cup still elude?

code goad

Am I a code that goads
within but without
here but from there
as I puzzle about?
what makes a man tick
is it worth it to ponder?
or grow and accept
that we small
bear the presence
of Him who sees all,
as the colour cast off
from the light prism split,
as all that you call
but see and won't be
is me; a rather odd bit.

of big bangs and laboratory life sparks

old fool,
spouting your theorem
of bangs and sparks,
that life would walk itself
from star dust to you

standing there
in your irreducible glory,
using that very essence
which your mirror-glass eyes
reflect back at me,
to see not you but me standing there,
who would push you
into your willing precipice,
that you might fall into the arms
of that which you deny

but lo hear the Word,
the quiet call of faith,
lest you slip through the fingers
that you prise apart by your wilfulness,
born of your stubborn pride

On the glorious and somewhat mystifying act of spontaneous and unassisted evolution

monkey does as monkey sees
swinging on old snakey's tree,
apples falling on the ground
monkey thinks his soul is found

monkey looks up to the stars
calls the people from afar,
people come and take a look
as monkey wiggles down the hook

people grab at what they please
on monkey's palm is snakey's grease,
for a swing and then a lunch
he leads the people, take a crunch

people do as monkey sees
wriggly little snake is pleased,
as people fall upon the ground
dying with those choking sounds

Evangazeal

one in one around the tree
sniffing for uncertainty,
resting now beneath the boughs
he's up there still so I will prowl

until he comes on down to me
and joins me for a little tea,
his smile is painted like the day
in time with me he'll pray and pay

and when I finally let him be
maybe then the Lord he'll see,
and if he doesn't I'd like to bet
more shakes will fill the flushing net

The Shepherds of Faust

A marriage of convenience I would call it;
that relationship of parallel lines
or of parallel lives,
whereby the shepherd walks with the sheep
in the shadows of the mount
and by his presence
does the subtle death begin,
that unconscious crawl
of the fall of value set
in the heart if not the mind.

He should call them from the light of the sun,
to go in search of that which is lost
as a walk to and fro,
the sinning sheep
upon his shoulders borne,
and to the light return—
for to go and to stay
in that collusion with Faust,
is the sure death in time
by those thousand short steps.

barbed arrows

The barbed arrow of communication
shot from the bow of Him who,
for one moment possible as a cupid,
of His own will did He write upon it
the words I sought,

to feel not the fleeting penetration
but deep did it drive
into the artesian tap of my soul,
longing for that which was buried
but only from sweat pooled
came the reflection,
so to see the form of experiential prayer;
the might of which dwells hidden
in the dreams of men.

My Biblical Brides

Must I stand on your doorstep
kind women of faith,
your door open wide
and in greeting you call my name.

As a child to your arms
and in your Father's love
do I see His word in your palms,
these hands that are His.

You who would lead this lost sheep
into all knowledge,
to sit him down at the hearth
of your understanding.

A warm cup of milk and the book of life
that saved you brides of Christ,
as I stare into the fire
but cannot speak and will not read.

No words from my heart will open your minds,
your house is mine,
your fire is warm;
take back your cup.

The Mass

Hallowed boards, polished anew,
the faithful tread
a spirit's substitute.
The pious enter, eyes cast aground,
iron pews full;
a holy sign.
On altar of stainless, biscotti laid down,
the host is ground
blood flows brown.
Liquid now, metamorphosis complete,
tongue's taste pure,
chemical's song unleashed.
New life within, this day renewed,
an evangelist's eyes see
colours untrue.
Finite for eternal, life's new vault,
to soothe the soul's void;
such forlorn hope.

the quickness test

To those that pass the quickness test, prostrate at the base
of the throne
the pilgrims lay their last address, and within the suffering rooms
of home
the bed of fate would soon reveal
which of those succumbed to hate and who is left in slow decay—
to feel the touch of one seems moot, yet who would follow
the lyrical flute
that draws the poor, the blind, and sick,
to pass that test of the door.
Could you discern the deliverance mores?

the meter

from the throng of this place
this time-confused home,
spoken of in books become
spewing from the secular throne
this lore that calmly sits astride
the mighty booms of material mind,
swinging to the worldly mores
and the meter of the techno-spore,
there comes a time when all becomes;
not now—we know there is no law
that sits upon us in our haste
to break the seal and find the taste

Bear Tidings

crawling through old London Town
the streets are dark
the houses brown,

and as I look into the grey
that wraps the sky
and shields the day,

I see my culture standing there,
was the genesis
came the bear,

that ate the world
and took its twin,
only Christian soldiers win,

'twas the expansion of the age,
as it rolls on
behold the cage.

Slumbering Seed

and what disturbs you, keepers of the safe?
that they who bow before him,
that they in their daily retinue
with their fasting and their war cry
of god
in the swirling mass of pilgrimage
to a far place;
would carry the scent, would carry the sense
of a walk to a hill, a scattering of seed
and of power in the One,
the cost of the journey so total and complete;
as the veil hides their form
has the western curtain fallen upon the true face
of that which you keep
in your safe?
does their war cry steel your blood?
do you yearn for battle yet?

upon the wasted heath

Is loneliness just life's persuasion
knocking at the gilded door?
Were the knights of childhood dreams
mere echoes returning from the poor?

Upon the strain of privilege
beneath the great sarcophagus,
within the stain of bloody wine
lies the deepest part of us.

That which knocks in the dead of night
upon the door of gold,
a shining path unto the plight;
so few are counted bold.

Enough to pass the door and run
onto the wasted heath,
enough to utter unto the world;
draw your conscience from its sheath.

Escape and Redemption

I went to sea
I fled to sea
on high wings of aluminium foil,

Sea black
Sky black
kissed, and I became their son,
and everywhere I looked was me;
high above the finite wash,
deep beneath the infinite silence.

So I wept
behind my poker-hand face,
and as I dreamt
those lies flew from their landlocked prison
and as they soared with me
they sang
as black doves on the night wing,
settling as ashes fall,

Their release
releasing me;

To be free above the finite wash,
To be still
beneath the infinite hand
of God.

III
LIGHT

You, Father

You are all
and I am none.

That I would carry your name
upon my forehead

and that which was foretold
in the books that you keep
at the centre of things

would announce to the world,
that which has become;

that I am yours,
and beside you
there is none.

On Being 40 and a Bit

Some say time is as the thief,
a moment's lapse, a life is gone,
years blend as sand grains,
that first red tinge crowns the blue horizon.

But I say we are as thieves of time,
for time no friends nor enmity knows,
just an ocean's great current
walking the sun's path to horizon's embrace.

Theft is as a lack of being,
the hollow canoe, drifting ever only,
to never strike across the current
or cast and harness great bounty from the deep.

But be sure, horizon's face will turn dark blue,
the sun's race will be won,
an ocean's grasp is but too sure;
and the time of eternity's true face will have come.

JC

And how did those hands
created within the common womb,

those Carpenter's hands
come to hold creation so?

As iron pierced flesh,
what spirit flowed
with the red blood of that man?

Which spirit did so infect
and spread
and would not stop?

Tell me how, this faint echo
of one life, one death?

Tell me why
it is here now?

And do you hear how,
can you stop
and with me listen now?

My Father's Den

Reaching pillars; how they march on shoulders' arches borne
held high to breathe the notes of the faithful as they pray.

Melodious voices rise on thermals of their love in praise of Him
as deep shadow soothes the dappled light laid low across the sanctum red.

A Sunday life, a weeks of ills, of birth and death by altar stone,
the pews knelt down upon the ground on which the bricks raised up on high.

This place of peace, this holy space where candles cast their own insight,
my Father's den, this place within; will you drink my life of sin?

Plain Me

I am plain,
I am plain,
could it be that I could convince myself?

Could it be that I could convince you?
That the shell is left,
like the Shucker's by-product

The soft corruptible part
taken,
by the knife

Only calcium left,
deflector shield,
krypton cloak;

Now that I am plain
I may be like
that I AM

In plainness I triumph,
for that which was first
is now made last

My last self
now made first;
this victory is truth.

my cup, His cup, my cup

take this cup from me He said,
take it from me Father;

such a small cup mine,
the comparative sip,
to look at the fluid within
calm and clear,
a small circle of reflection,
just a part of my soul
stares back at me;

then a quick swirl
and I'm lost in the current
of taste; is it bitter
like His?
as he lay face down
in the sands
that drew water from His body
into this vessel of mine;

potion of the godhead,
drink it quickly—
then let the drug of life behold

Ungrateful Sod

You took them
My gifts to you
He said

You took them
As the peasant
Humble

Father
I will sing to you
As I sow

So you worked those fields
With his tools
And you grew

In those eyes
That washed over you
Your crop

And you thought
These are,
These are mine

I am king
And you drank those praises
Meant for him

You whose girth swelled
From his fields,
From his plough—

Now sit down in your field
Place your tools
At his feet

And sing praise
As the peasant
Sing praise

Obituary

count them up;
the words of your obituary
are they long and eloquent?

do they flow from the mouths
of the mourning
as the wine of your life
flowed like blood
from the palms
that turned towards the iron pierce
of rejection?

do your words
count the times you stood
and would not bow
your head
to those who would scorn
your path?

make them short
these words your clothes cast aside,
naked
to the voices
that speak the truths of your times,

words of love
words of faith
hear them now,
hear them now.

mighty pens and worthy men

take it up
you mighty men
rise and feel the metal
of the singing pen,
upon the pages found
in great journals told
sear a line of truth
bring the wheat to the fold,
and set you to the field
bowing down before the Lord
scythe the righteous path
your pen singing to the Word,
and at the reaping time
lay down the fountain sword
and under the harvest moon
set a light to the hoard
left remaining in the field
as stubble under foot
bid no sad farewell
Death come—your burning loot

mountain man

mountain-top man,
how you sing
His praises
from the point
of high advantage

that we may see
you,
your word
is your life;
a beacon
in the night,
and the works
of your hands
are humble,
they are His
these hands
with which
you pray
and you cup
over your mouth
as you shout
His name

mountain-top man,
call us up,
who would whisper
in the valleys,
who know His name
and hide
in the shadows
of the peaks
on which you stand—
call us up

Sandflies

we're moving so quickly that we never freeze
in the very spot we're in,
to look around at the trees,
markers of our neighbourhoods
lining and defining,
tall as Greek ceremonial guards;
those absorbers of time
as we brush against them as sandflies,
children climb precariously to lateral limbs
wooden castles where imaginations run wild
of pirates and secret clubs,
no adults within;

our shady evergreens
leaving washing lines stranded
spouting overflowing
helpless and lint-clogged,
a river of development flowing around
as rocks caught in a flash flood;

to be a part or a parcel,
do we stop by our sentinels
as our lives tumble down
our own river beds
to find some deep blue end
and rest?

Amelia's poem

When I look to the sea green,
that contrasts with sky blue,
framed by Harakeke seed heads from below,
by cloud shapes
beckoning imagination games from above

I see the green of hazel mix
in my daughter's eyes

Then in my mind I see;
the like elements,
the purposeful will
of the common hand

And I think that
they are both gifts most beautiful.

Sun Lapse

A light without heat bathes my face,
that perfect moment comes

The sun floating
obliterates the mountains below
in a pall of golden mist

The eternal farewell

Plains become a dance floor,
hedgerows and shelterbelts alive
dark partners fall long at their feet

I inhale the golden light

An illusion of a motionless state,
that trickery wrought through the lingering day
is exposed now

As the mountains eclipse
their falling crown

Before night breathes and claims this day

It is hers now
And it is long

Mute Kiss

I stand mute
as a mule
full of muscle
bound
by your harness
and a rope
of the tethering kind
to the post
of your expectation
upon the earth
of your consultation,
paid for
in those pieces of silver
minted
in that moment
with a kiss,

sweet kiss
upon the cheek
of the One,
only in innocence spoken.

Mainstream

I hacked at the mooring line;

the one that held me fast
to the stolid ground
of the bank
to which I'd become rather attached.

And a little movement
heralded my escape
in that slow current
that pulled at my bow
and directed my prow.

And it was the bank moving,
it was not me,
for I had become centre
and it the circumference of the world
to which I now belonged.

And I longed for the earth
between my clenched fists,

but the bank was gathering speed,

for my time had come,

and the flow of the Lord
was so swift and serene,
that I knew at last
I'd answered His call.

prism man

I was thinking that there
must be something more,
an Aladdin's key
to unlock the door,
a room beyond this
a dimension foretold,
a foot in each world
a place to unfold,
and when it has taken
the predestined man
will he leave the un-lit
for the rainbow-laced land?
to sing with the ones
who stood on the hill
where a white beam of light
split the prism of will.

The Father

you thought the sky blue
all that I see
and feel
and know is you

you are the sky blue
all that I hear
all that I care
is you

you are the night blue,
black is the blue
you paint over day
the black is you

you are the night
the black is still true
yet in the last light,
all, Father, is you

Within and Without

In emptiness I know
of a space so replete
if I fell today
into the changeless sleep,

and awoke on the shores
of a glass distant sea
there in the twilight
would I await to see,

if the vessel I'd left
had kept any hint
of the contents that burned
before they were lit,

and set to the flame
a consuming tongue,
a fire so intense
it seared as the sun,

and charred the vessel
inside of the keep
so creating a space
that was empty; replete.

Now would any self
remain of me
on the beautiful shores
of the changeless sea?

and as I stepped out
into the twilight
lo the gaze of the Godhead
with my form now without.

a reasoning season

I know that faith
must follow reason
and reason
must question.

But when I question
you so
I find the limits
to that reason.

And when I thus fail
your will is the cushion
on which I gladly rest
my head for a season.

I can no more understand you
than the gadfly the man;
reason may lead faith
but faith transcends reason.

New Zealand Peace Poem

peace be with you
peace be with me
peace be with me
and this land on the sea

love be with you
love be with me
love be with me
and this land floating free

joy be with you
joy be with me
joy be with me
and this land God can see

God be with you
God be with me
God be with me
and this land He set free

In the now

And who would experience
with me
the white marble halls
of tranquility?
yet golden sands
with blue beach chairs
see the life of man
forsake the cares.

Of struggle in
the quickness lane
to earn the passage
to leave the pain;
life in two parts
one dark, one light
with hell the first,
the second delight.

But walk with me
please, if you would
the two separate
come eternal good;
for life within
the veil of Christ,
small duties pass
without disgrace.

And golden sands
with blue beach chairs
exist within;
there is no fear,
and beyond all this
low mortal toil
lie marble halls,
time's priceless call.

Wisdom Found

To have all
Is to have nothing
Nothing at all

To have less
Is to have more
It is to be blessed

To have known
To have lost
Is to have found

To have known
Is to keep
In faith replete

I have looked
I have lost
I find
Now I'm found

Angel, mourn

Will the angels sing
when darkness falls
on the final minutes
of my days of delight?

Or will they fold their wings
and look away?

My pilots, my guides,
sentenced to watch
the newsreel
of my life,

to walk within the screen,
the characters
unblinking
at their pass.

And does my judgement cause them
to fear,
or does God whisper such things
in their ears so that they know,

of what will come to pass
as they kneel at the bed
of the last
long sleep?

And what of my soul,
will they cradle it so
on the journey
to the halls of righteousness?

And will their test be like mine
the sprint,
or as the fruit ripens long;
and will they start to sing?

How I hope the angels will know
to unfold their wings.

The Platform

Speak to me of the last rainfall
Speak to me of the dusk
Speak to me of a journey near past;
From this platform death departs.

A life, a spark, one brief light
upon the velvet blue
a whisper close upon His lips
a mirage on the desert's hue.

Not with regret nor apology
a life spent to completion
the timing right to pass this fold
onto the New Jerusalem.

I've felt this world, its suffering
as a father of its children
I've wrought what joy a human could;
I may no longer question.

An unseen force has seen me through
these lonely corridors
the hand that guides has mystified
but now opens one last door.

Into the arms of He who waits
I've walked the line of faith
with grace and mercy upon His breath
He holds me now; I'm safe.

Look, Here Comes that Fool

"For the word of the cross is foolishness to those who are perishing, but to us who are being saved it is the power of God."

—St Paul, 1 Cor 1:18 (NASB)

Harbor of Dreams

Father, you know we harbor
these dreams
in our hearts true.
Hidden beneath
the layers of the day,
our scales of iron
would deflect the world of our placement,
that we would be alone with you
in the quiet spaces within.
And these dreams
that we carefully raise
would grow and become bold
and rail against the confinement
of our fears.

Father, you know we harbor
these dreams
in our hearts deep.
Where we may hold a mirror
to the face of Your Spirit
and in imitation
fly, through the world of our placement
as great birds of light,
and graciousness would fall
from our coat of feathers
to lie at the feet
of those we fear;
who through their simple indifference
would cause us to cower
in the far places of our hearts,
and tell our dreams, no.

The Triangle

The walls you build for me Father,
are they to keep the world out
or do they keep me within
a garden of your will?

Your thoughts and your Word
spring like flowers underfoot,
as I tread through the meadows
I tend within these, your three walls.

And shall I look out from this haven
with scorn,
or shall I beckon these, my brothers and sisters
to come within your Trinity?

And sit with me,
encircled by the three in one.
That never ending triangle
of Father, Spirit and Eternal Son.

A Tree of Life

Pieces of me fall, drifting to the ground,
they were once my cover.

A beautiful summer coat of green
became gold as the sun dipped,
how she runs from your hand to hand
lower still.

And was this long autumn
ample warning?

Did you coax me from my mid-summer dreams
as the children laughed and played beneath me?

Where have they gone
my little ones;
called inside to their mother's arms?

But me
remember me,
my coat upon the ground
you see me now stricken and bare;
was I not your friend too?

Oh Father, raise the sun upon me once more
that I might know your warmth
and they could return
my little ones,
to the shade of my summer boughs.

my Son

It is in the quiet times
that I can no longer run from the thought of you;
that image, like a sheet, white
enshrouds me
becoming my gown
that I would wear if I could just for once
step through the hours of each day
in your image, my Son.

But that gown falls from narrow shoulders
and lies upon the ground,
yet not like yours which was taken from you,
leaving the man alone with His Father.

No, mine is cast down by my own thoughts,
for you see my Son
I lose my courage when the noise begins again,
I lose that focus, that strength
that holds my enshrouding gown
in those quiet times.

And what would I give
to be able to hold it close,
my shield, my defense
as I stride in my mind
through the streets of this city, a man
like you my Son—

alone, and with His Father.

Gentle Tide

What gentle persuasion of yours
is this, Father?
met by light steps
as I dance along the shoreline
your breath as the tide,
would you beckon me come out
into those wide open spaces
where sky and earth as sea meet
and become in the color of your eye
blue, as I might sail
in an ocean of teeming life—

Angelfish move to the rhythm of the currents
of your mind
and in that mind's eye
do you see me now?
on the threshold of your ocean long is my wait
lest the pull of the tide
mighty as it is,
would render this will obsolete—
Who am I to give you
that which could not return?
afraid am I to return
that which you would give—

What gentle persuasion
of yours
is this, Father?

the man

How weary I am of foot,
from this pilgrimage
to the base of a cross,
set upon a hill
I did not expect to find,
thinking it but a stroll,
my head held high and
borne of regal countenance,
as friends and equals
yes my Lord I would come
on my terms, you know me
did I seek to entertain
the gracious gesture
I would see shining
in the glory of your Father's light,
thinking it but a little thing,
'til I realized, yes
I could see you now
hung high upon that place,
your body broken and torn;
for me,

Behold the man.

And at my shoulders
the pilgrims of time
jostled for their places at your feet;
time came and went,
sat with me still
and was gone,
my legs weary from the climb,
worn to the knees
upon which I was found
in your presence;
afraid now to raise my eyes,
lest you saw how poorly I came.

The Name

I call your name
And you are there,
In the night sky
Draped in robes of velvet black;
Countless stars adorn your head
And you are mine
And your name is truth
And your name is Jesus

I call your name
And you are there,
Upon the night sea
Draped in robes of velvet blue;
The moonlight adorns your body
And you are ours
And your name is Jesus
And your name is man

I call your name
And you are there,
In my mind behind eyes shut
Draped in robes of scarlet red,
And you are your own self
And the light of truth
Adorns your spirit,
And your name is man
And your name,
it is God

Silence

The morning silence sits at my table
and wraps itself around my imagination
like a great snake of intertwining curves,
to choke from my memory those sweet young voices
of daybreak and dreams
and nights spent in the sanctum of love's hold;
the morning song that rekindled my cold heart
and burned my soul deep,
to carry that name upon my breast,
the name of father
in which I was Your son
and in Your image was I made whole;
in their sweet need.

The Loom

On snow-encased slopes
Is my life found of wont
Softly tread
Softly tread
These steep lanes of ice,
As weary legs rise
And fall with the moons
Does my way rise and pull
As silk on the loom,
That's it, will I cry
The Lord wait to see
If I pick it up lo
This burden of being,
And cast it on high
For eagles set free
Who carry it swiftly
To white mountains far,
Where my Lord and his Word
Silhouette the night sky.

Closed dwellings

How they prayed
I once read of old,
that You would smite
the enemies of Israel,

Your sword raised, Your Word mighty,
oh God of wrath
how they must have adored You
in battle;

Yet how we know You now;
Your face love and Your shield held high
as mercy, Your Son, the sword of truth
would penetrate the heart—

Now the enemy has hidden within
the fields of flowers remember,
that sacrifice of the heart
laid before the God of peace—

What armistice is this in our souls?
quiet be the surge of armies
that break upon
the capstone of truth.

And all this they sought of You,
we seek now
in the closed rooms of our dwellings,
far from the searching gaze

of our kind.

My head upon the earth

And you flew with me
Lord God,
as I walked the high passes
of your creation,
there, not through my own efforts,
how you called me forth
to those exalted heights
as my eyes saw all there was to see
in this world.
And you surrounded me
with your majesty,
your spirit became all that I touched
and could know.

And you kneel with me
Lord God,
as I rest my head on the earth
of my belonging;
am I there at the end
of all that you would share.
Take my hand.
Take my hand.
And lay me down to sleep
in my trust, my faith trust,
will I know your face,
your beautiful smile will embrace
when I awake in the place
of your choosing.

the Night Birds

Cry of the night birds,
still my soul,
alone am I, in this small cabin
set upon the plains of consciousness;
I have walked so many miles,
how I've heralded
the glad tidings
above the noon sway of wheat.

As my day came and left
did I flee to this place,
to cower from those callers
that stalk and would seek
my last treasure,
yes daylight my shield
has laid down her time.

Oh cry of the night birds
how you taunt my mortal efforts
to seek the Harvester,

See not my small yield oh Lord,
pray count my lonely steps.

those who cry

Tell me of patience
born in the mouths
of those who cry silence,
for the small beast upon the stone. . .
do voices like echoes of sin
march two and two
to lay down in kind
that you would be set free—
Come, wait no more,
let silence clean the soul,
for the marionette's master
would lay his hands still
in search of patience
born in the mouths
of those who cry;
My Lord.

Dark Mask

When the still-dawn arises
like the waking one of dreams
walking the yards of the dust people.
Know my call, Lord God,
how you left me there
in my night of walking sleeplessness.
How I clawed at your dark mask;
you would not listen
to my demand for light's embrace.

That you would leave me
to stumble this pitiless path
of drunken toil.
Dark face of light
who hides in Your glorious realms,
You stood your servant still.
And in that lightless hour
before the still-dawn of dreams,
came the fall of ancestral hope.

On the Altar of Debt

Singing ears,
how you chime like the bells
of churches found in old cities
of the rhymes of my young days;
such places of fables
and memories born
on the sweet pages of life,
with a moral and a lesson
of tidy days of sin and succession,
to the march of the catechism
and the conditioning font of lines
spent after the terminal tone of day.

Singing ears,
do you chant a rhythm
to the sway of my soul,
back and forth but away
to the altar of debt;
and now the chimes
be the warning cry of hosts,
that within the body
are laid long nails of iron,
and soon will the church bells
ring out for these ears,
silenced in the sleep of night.

Small Hands

I curse these hands of small import
Laid low,
As meaninglessness dances
And chants before my eyes
And ears;
How I look at the ones
Blessed in abundance
Of some one small part
Of us;

They rise above the mist
Of lives lived in long intervals,
Between pieces
Of silver
Dancing across a floor
In that betrayal of all time,
And of our times;
Be our quiet reward for these
Ungrateful ways.

Ice Dance

You danced with me Lord on the white rinks of life;
our courtship was not smooth, how you chose your ways well,
haughty and anxious as I was and slewed your love
time and time on;
my sharp embrace of conditions carried
close to my heart, my own great wall
to keep the seething hordes of your spirit at bay,
your armies sent crashing against the crystalline walls,
still your dance in circular motion
around ever around
the object of your devotion;

worthiness born not of woman nor action nor word nor thought
but of grace bestowed upon the violent one hidden
within the snaking walls of ice,
that once melted to the touch of mercy;

yes I danced with you Lord
as our love
scribed the ice with patterns copied to white pages
in journals,
telling of my devotion to you
and this small gift of thanks.

Brother

I died for you today brother,
and did you hear
my breath trace the path of a hiss
from taut lips,
did you see in my eyes
the sharp and cold touch of want,
and did you know
for what I give to you brother
to lay at your tombstone rolled,
silent partner
of the fruit-laden gardens
in which I slay this being,
daily;
how I seek the cool dust
in these times,
to be wrapped in a cloak of wood
and within the earthen womb,
that the slain one might fly
to your shoulder;
I drink the dark blood
of filial denial.

Grey Cat

I found myself one day
in the lucid light of dawn dreams,
with grey cat stealth
I sprung upon my own self-consciousness
a trap,
set in the bright days
of my wandering search
here and there,
where the observation would at once render
the goal beyond the reach
of my mind.

Yes, I found myself one day
in that place between the worlds,

where consciousness lost its cause
and left me servile,
to the loving admonitions
and chorus
of the divine song.

The Innocents

What tales told
by small ones with bright eyes,
glistening in the fond hue of spring;

what lives lived
before their time in young minds
where castle walls are built
stone upon stone
of hope and expectation;

and what like of stone
around the necks of those
who would take these walls
and paint them black,
with sorrow and with pain,
cast dull before bright eyes;

a stone the weight
of exploitation's want,
that would not tarry
till it found its home
in the very deep places of hell.

Upon the Dry Ground

Do choices fall
upon ears deaf
to the distant call of
voices, born in the primal mind
of all?

Do those closest
to the angels of evangelism,
and within their own homes,
turn their cheek
from the blows that would fall
in loving kind,
as His cheek turned
in mercy found
through those dark hours?

And if choices fall
as rain upon the parched
lips of time,
to be spat
upon dry ground;
would such selfish ones
then be lost
to the last muster
of those
He calls His own?

The Autumn of Thorns

Come, the days of fair autumn frost,
good friends,
for he was with you
but a short while.

Come, the time
of decisions molded
from the clay of the earth
on which we stand.

Come, gaze into a limitless heaven,
the reaches of which cause our mind
to round on itself,
suffer its own failure to know.

Come, the scales of justice
that weigh the clay
with all above
in the following ides of winter snow.

Come, the dagger of thorns, woven
into the low crown of betrayal,
and driven deep
into the brow of mercy.

The Watchers

Lone is the dark wolf
who stands at my gate,
his vigil in the night times
of my day dreams
the spirit shadow
of his lust in the day times
of my night dreams.

Lone is the dark wolf,
set sentry by the one
who would wander the earth
of fallow desire,
was he cast behind
the beautiful One
set low by His own will,
that no latch need open
to the dark watchers
of the gates to our souls.

Alone and with the Many

I sit alone with the many
of a kind
I do not seek
and cannot see,
for they are forsaken
to me
in my new cloak
of colors painted
in the eye
of my Lord's mind.

I sit replete
in the company
of the Author
of new times;
upon me the spirit
fell
and continued
to the ground,
and when I arose
I was no more
in the company
of these fellows,
who see all
and nothing at all,
in the faces
of their own.

The Crypt

I touched your feet
yes they were cold and chipped,
the colors faded
from the light
that had crept
even to this dark corner.

I touched your feet
and chanced to glance
at your face; a death-mask frozen,
this work of the sculptor's hand
clumsy
beside my vision
of your long loving self.

I touched your feet
at once meek and yet bold,
and this small movement
became the touch of the child
I knew in the like
of my mother Mary's arms.

I touched you Lord
and as my hand stretched back
those thousand or two years,
I was at one with the apostles
whose countenance
I'd consigned to pages I could edit
at the walk of my will.

I touched your feet
for the first time today,
and found my place
in a small crypt
behind the disciplined march
of the pews,
and in the midst of the conditioned
did I become unconditional
in self-defeat of grace bestowed.

Mark the Man

Mark me the man
who placed his body
as a dam of flesh,
held to that written in the sand,
and shattered before the flood tides
of persecution.

Mark me the man
laid down by the banks
of a quiet stream,
broken at once lifted
and cradled in the arms
of my loving parents three,
who mark me the son
who has nothing
that is not of his Father.

Weeping of the Boughs

I looked upon the tree of life
quietly mourning
my time of strife,
upon its laden branches borne
the slowly waking
mind of dawn,
walk me through the midnight hours
when all was lost
my time devoured,
all these promises of youth
the memories float
their power to soothe,
lost within the first dawn light
another day
began the fight,
to walk beneath its weeping boughs
and take the bread
my demons prowl,
no, place it in my languid mouth
its goodness flows
for me to shout
its glory by another name
swallow now,
forsake the pain.

Without Cause

Conscience without cause
sits splayed upon the ground,
regarding me with large round eyes
of worldly account,
bottled tightly and plied
with moral preservative,
I shall place it on a shelf
in my pantry,
along with my earthquake survival kit,
that it may be
for a dinner table discussion,
or a rainy day,
when death weeps
on the garden parties
of good people.

Gravity

Bitter fruit
Falls from the tree,
Tree of life
Tree of strife,
Gravity will help me see
Oh bitter fruit
Don't fall on me

Cold at your side

My your lips are ice
sweet thing,
you are not yourself
or are you at once your own,
save my fine advice
for another day
to come,
when your lips will lie truly
cold
at your side.

a Foundling

I must go to the hard places
and dwell therein.
In my life of many colors
do I shine like the cuckoo
and seek in you
the loving incubation
of my own foundling,
will you find him
borne in your own desires;

my wish,
my eternal kiss of life,
that stirred that fine day
on the pages
that caressed your wax heart.

the Silicon Robe

Lines of grief drift
in wayward passage
across the suffering face
of a church forsaken
by her kin,
stood still alone,
clothed in nothing
but the light
of the One
who stood like them
naked,
at humanity's edge;

Rain the blows
of bitter kind
upon the turning cheek
of sacrifice,
and bid us farewell,
who know nothing
but fine robes of silicon
and our words of comfort
dipped in sour wine.

of Crumbs and Hope Itself

Scatter me seed
that I would crawl
upon your earth
and find them one by one;
I will plant
the tree of life.

Cast me crumbs
from the loaf of the table,
find the floor of righteousness
that I would crawl
and gather them one on one;
I will make
the bread of life.

Scatter me hope
upon the heart-boards
in long rooms of congregation,
that I would kneel
with blind tears of joy;
I will make it
in the image of my faith,
and hope itself will be
the body of my life.

To Rise

I have no fear
of these times,
that surround me
as junkyard dogs.

I need only pull
my cloak tightly
around me,
as my Christian shield.

I am as nothing
safe,
within a carapace
of your indifference
to the suffering
of this world.

And if I opened
my cloak
and you were to slay me,
I would only arise
at the third passing
of the sun,
and you would see me
in her warm morning light,
and you would know me
in the shadow
of your own despair.

The Light

She walks before me
in the night
softly, slowly,
new starlight,
from her lantern
held with care,
she lights the way
dispels my fears,
she is my angel
the guiding one;
she asks no favor
lives as the Son;
her hand is old
and withered now
for it was taken
from the plough,
the fields she tended
by midday sun,
her back is bent
the burdens come;
but beauty stalks
her grey-streaked hair
and beauty walks
without life's fear,
for light is not
the lantern's preserve;
light the eyes
the Spirit's Word; it
shines now from
her inner being,
she is the light
my eyes have seen.

An Apportionment

When two angels cry,
think you dark things,
upon wing have they flown
upon will have they shown,
your apportionment of
petit crawling grace
based on the sum
of low listless faith;

now you who would cry,
"Good angels
to my side,"

and with none seen around
the place you have found,
to sleep night away
eternal dark claims,
no awakening now...
to dust your hope clings.

the Author

He is the Author
of our lives.
He writes the script
upon white pages
in the manner of His choosing.

Our times are but
the stroke of His pen
and He will turn
these pages at His will.

And as the ink dries,
the letters of our lives
are for all to read
in these quiet days.

Our marks upon the face
of our one time
are stored and treasured,
and will stand
as the letters of love
in the annals of all times,
and in these times of all.

Soul Cry

Father, did you read the mime
of my lips, how they moved
as I sought your Word,
yet nothing came from this mouth
for there is no word
and there is no sound
that could speak of my need,
trapped bird in the cage
of inadequacy,
my long soul cry,
this inability to reach out
in a way
that would let you know,
could let you see,
my need for you at this moment;
I am lost within the vessel
you gave me;
tear down these bars
and raise my voice on high
that you would hear my cry,
that you would see my despair,
that you would know me in this hour

but you know me in this hour.

tattered me

Father, in moments such as these
I am bare before you,
the remnants of my pride,
tattered garments of gold
that glittered
in the days of sunlight
I enjoyed without thought
of how and where I came
to be in the presence
of those things that are yours;
seek not the maker
that the sun would set
and with it all purpose,
bare before you
am I
on this bed
in the rest of quiet despair.

Still

Father, still, I am here
among the great trees of your forests,
still in body and mind
but not in heart nor soul
which heave and strain, set to break
upon the high winds of choice,
that would fell tall trees of shallow root
and lay the ground bare;
but those that would stand
still as me,
grow stronger ever upwards,
the soaring ones call,
a will of iron heart and soul of steel
set in long days of the wild call of sin,
set for You
and the great tasks of eternity,
that wait patiently ahead.

Raw Metal

Father, Yours is the blacksmith's
roughened hand,
how Your forge seared
as raw metal sang
in pain,
white hot across the coals
of self-denial,
slowly shaped, ever drawn long
is the blade,
now cooled and sharpened
on the weary stone of patience,
long days to and fro
and the luster that shines
will blind the idle ones
with Your glory,
as this sword in Your hand
scythes the fields of righteousness;
in these days was I made,
in those days will I come,
in Your name
I will come
and in Your power
they will know me.

Our Lord

Our Lord is beautiful;
as we kneel at the door
of His dwelling place
and ask
that we may enter;
but He has already
opened the door,
and stands before us
His arms open in welcome
as He calls us come
before we thought to ask.
And His smile
tells our hearts
of His love,
and His embrace
tells our souls
of our salvation.
And we enter
that we may know, in truth;
how beautiful
is the face
of Our Lord.

The Risen One

He is risen, friends,
come cradle your souls
upon His wings
spread
across the day-sky light,
Come soar
upon His mantle of stars
within the velvet hue
of the night-sky light,

Come ride
the great currents of salvation
up
into the arms
of His Father's might,

Come see
His face
framed by the hosts of perfection
robed in brilliant white,

He is risen, friends,
come know of life
and taste the sweetness
of this one true delight.

Wooden Eagle

Place him to the left;
the eagle that hath never flown,
place him to the right;
the preacher that hath never known,
place him in the seat of trivia;
the Lord whose Word disowned.
Oh sing to Him today
and be on your merry way,
to your lives of ritual mime,
best this life
a death in time.

East of here

Sinners of the church
look east,
cast aside your silk
and your pearls.
From the high Western citadel
you gaze
upon the narrow streets
of Islam;
where your brothers
walk His path,
where your sisters
cry out His name,
rough cloth upon their backs;
scourged.
Peel open the pages of flesh
on which He writes His name.
Now take your silk
and bind these wounds
as His,
and salve your consciences
before the gaze
of hosts;
that they would know
your lowly name,
and too your latent shame.

On Gentle Slopes

You, who build your houses
on the hill;
my Father watches you.
You, who look across
the plains of low suffering,
and care not
but for your own feet,
high above the damp touch
of need;
my Father listens for you.
For it is only
in your midnight restlessness,
when sleep departs from
the reach of human will,
that the first small cry
of the damned
would reach His ears,
and tell Him
of the secrets
locked in your closed hearts.

To Reflect the Light

Father, I will worship You;
I desire to live in Your love
through Your mercy
and by Your grace.
I would make this body
the hearth of Your spirit.
I would make this mind
the lone pages of Your script.
I would make this soul
reflect the light
of the glory of Your Word,
even to a world-in-waiting.
Father, I will use my hands
as the earth hands of Jesus,
as they reach
through the curtains
of time.
I will use this heart
to feel Christ's pain,
as wounds bound by rough cloth,
and stained in the blood of wine.
Father, I will lay myself bare
by the high altars
of heaven.
I will lay myself low
before the feet
of the divine Son,
Who is Your Word and Your own kin.

Father, I will worship You
because this is truth.
Father, I will worship You
because this is happiness.
Father, in my worship of You,
I am as one whole
in the image You created of me,
before my time began.

a Saving Love

Father
Save me,
I am my own self
only when I am
of yourself,
I will not confront your enemies
by my own pride,
but I will immerse myself
in your glory
and that will be their defeat.

I will not live as the child of fear
but as the brother of hope;

Hope in your faithfulness
to my cause,
hope in your gracious presence
in my days,
and hope in your saving love,
through my long nights.

Seconds for Thoughts

What is the man who asks
and who seeks
in the dead arms of night,
for kingdoms born in the hearts
of his fellows?

who says—Lord
take it all
and thresh with Your own hands,
that the wheat of harvest come
through a life fulfilled
in You;

Then what is the man
who sees the dark shadow
of death upon his fields?
as the gaze of the iniquitous one
falls upon harvest times
of gold;

and knows his own fear?

of thoughtless hope

You, down by the river,
wash your clothes with care.
Launder and press them
between the hotplates
of love.

Present yourself new and clean,
and I will see you in the line
that winds its merry way
towards the seat of
judgement.

Can you feel it;
the power of the throne
of knowledge,
of all your little deeds?

Happy one,
how you play
with your toys of summer delight;
lo the queue grows short
and the fabric long.

Cloth too well beaten
on the rocks
of thoughtless hope.

Cloth too well worn
on the back
of selfish want.

Cloth too thin to hide
the motive
from the deed.

That Fool

Look, here comes that dreamer,
unfit in his own skin.
Let his head seek
those high realms of light
that we might pull his feet
to this earth,
should his dreams
spill out
for all to see.

Look, here comes that fool.
See them now
upon the ground,
that we may laugh
at those things
he dreamed.
Let his feet go
so he might float away
in the arms of hosts;
the loan company
of innocents and fools.

Look, here comes that dreamer.
He is gone now.
So what became
of those things
cast into the pit
of his brothers' scorn?
Was the worth
of treasure
found
in a trampled cloak of color,
and raised by the hands
of God,
to be hung high on the shoulders
of fools?

The Autumn Crypt

I kissed the cross
that autumn day,
the color of my lips
sang golden brown
and faithful red,

as old friend nature
laid me down
beneath her crypt
of summer leaf,

how those memories
danced the setting day
on the long sighs of angels,
who stood too near
to think myself alone.

And upon the gentle
earthen throne
as I kissed the cross
that autumn day,

in the lukewarm wash
of pastel bled,
I set my heart to allay
its worries and its cares,

I danced with them all
on the swirling autumn breeze,
and was gone;

my resting place,
cast beneath the feet
of children,
in their time of play,
on that last color day.

Changing of Ways

From lone flaming bush, voice on the air
lay down your will,
forsake all the cares.
To finding the voice, deep hidden within
a lifetime of searching;
nothing given.

Away to the host, impeccable wares
away to the shell
that wishes to hear.
The guidance and words, the Father of all
the help and the taste;
heaven forestalled.

Where brilliant white beings will govern with love
and take forth the people,
the Godhead above.
And present the new person, the source of that love
and seated to the right
the One with the dove.

Upon His own lap, hands turned to bear
the source of salvation,
scars, He will share
with children who bow before Him in space
and accept from the Father
a heavenly grace.

And in service go forth, long ranks of hosts
to share with the angels
the spirit of those,
who sought and would seek and never stop trying
with no burning bush;
the voice that is crying.

To be heard and obeyed, through long lonely days
the lone voice that may count
in the changing of ways.

Seam of Coal

For those who love
too much,
for those whose feelings
run too deep
in that seam
of soul,
found
where there is no
place for darkness,
only that product
of union
between me and Thee—
there is no rest
on this planet
of sorrow;
the short nights
belie the presence
of that which
must become
not at all
and yet whole;
in those times
of light,
and in those times
of distant life.

of Talents

Take that log out,
take it out
man of means,
let it fall from your eye
bathed in the acid
of tears;
or was that your breath
as you lean
in their direction,
whose talents are few,
but who did not bury them
in the ground of contempt
as you were wont to do
with your many;
cast it out now
before the earth claims
your buried treasure
and leaves you as you are,
naked before your God,
with your log in your eye
and His words by your side.

Man of Rough Hands

The cock crowed at three
this clear morning;
man of rough hands
did you set your garment
aside?
and bid them see,
you are not of His flesh,
you are not of His kin,

how the morning chill
led you to this fire
but there was no warmth
of love in that place,
only scorn
that pierced the heel
and found the man inside,

all that glints and is at once
the steel of confidence,
worthless in that moment
of humankind,

your promises like sparks
hiss from the fire
and are gone,
the night swallowed them
before your disbelieving eyes;

eyes that saw the mercy
in the face of your Lord,
eyes that set in the rock
on which we have long stood,
and still that must become
more than our name;

for the cock crows once more;
it is the small hours,
and our hands are rough.

Fire

Fires of paradise,
consume me
in these times
of bitter deceit;

This illusory tale
that is my world of dreams
is pinned to the coat-tails
of men who do not know You;

See me in their wake
my life of countless days,
dancing to a somewhere tune
of spears
thrust deep into the flesh
of thieves;

I am he
who steals my own time
and gives it to those
who place its value
by their own measure
as null;

But by the light
of the fires of paradise
is my path
that You would take me,
and by extinction in the flame
of the Spirit, could I yet
be Yours.

A lonely peace

I have in my heart found
a space
for a delicate formation
of words
which may not part
my careful lips,

are they bound together
mute
by my decades
of clumsy speech;

and that essence
left
in this place of longing
is in its kind
a type of lonely peace.

a parallel thing

I am not here
but some other place,
a parallel
thing of two halves,
not at all equal
in measure,
for the one that
is not here—
he is held in greater esteem
than this man,
found little
in his own life.

little tongue

Flicker little tongue,
like the Serpent's;
how kind of you
to discuss my weary ways,
from your tree, pious snake,
as I see in your yellow eyes
the object
of my body's desire;
now tell your ruinous friends
all my secrets dear,
speak them
that they might know
my taste
upon the cold earthen airs;
still flicker little tongue,
but lo
you know
my time to come.

His Coming of Days

Still is the night
and deep calms the dawn
the crimson lies low
and the angels will mourn,
for the day of the beast
arises again
for the times of his feast;
so seeks out the shame,
now written across
the faces of those
whose love is the labor
as Spirit draws close,
whose backs bear the bond,
the demons lay hold
and ears hear the call
of Savior foretold;

By prophets who saw
in new morning sky
the promise of life
and then did they cry,
"Repent and prepare!"
for the coming of One
who through His own grace
will receive everyone,
who lives for His name
and lays down their load
and replaces it lo
with the yoke that was told;

But all of us now
have lived on in vain
as our planet, our lives
the precept of pain,
of times that were given
and since lost again
the gift of the age
the call to attain,
the joy found only
in Him who has been
as God and as man
the human foreseen;
but men did they die
while angels lived on
to see all our wares,
our material scorn;

We have lost Him since
in the haze of our ways
we have lost Him now
in the sins of our days,
yet must we find
our twisting way back
and yet must we bind
our cross to our back,
and carry it forth
through the days of the beast
and carry it now
as the sun leaves the East,
with colors of crimson
and the hope it relays
through the promise of Christ
in His coming of days.

The Cane

Let us go for a walk
the blind man said;
let us take all our ease
and the Lord to forget,
for I see all I need
and the need is in me
to know of the wares
of material tree,
and I'll walk
and I'll tap
the black hours away
for the rhythm of praying
is foreign to me;

At the end of the day
of life passed away
I'll look for the Lord
and He will see me
but His bright blessed ways
will be out of my reach
as His light and His grace
were dispensed to me free,
to be left on the ground
that I tapped with my tree,
the one made of good,
the one made of ease.

a place to call ourselves

I am not real
in this place
I call myself;
in silence
I lie before
the outer tongues
of Eden,
my companions of
sharp practices;
they do not see
their own home
as hell,
created in
image of idols
and cast in the alloys
of men;
still they know me
as real,
for I am in their place
a projection
of consciousness,
found in their dread
that life
was once hope—
in these days
of our last beginnings.

Crooked Hand

Come little teacher,
take your father's crooked hand
and lead him along your road;
a small road of memories
with a dusty heart
and lines that coil,
a road of travelling times
and small margins
between thee and beyond.

Come little hand,
soft with the hope
born of time in between
thee and me;
see you my withered claw
and wild-fed ways;
Oh my youth,
where treasure was dust
and dust it gave
the warm breath of life—
on this small road of memories;
how I sought your teaching ways.

two by two

Father, life and love you gave
Seek from me one debt repaid
And keep me safe from all that is
And with your will, may I forgive,
All who fail what I not am
Demanding ways my life has damned
To keep me separate from you
Now bring me back, two by two

As they came forth unto the ark
Let me be safe and set apart
Within your grace and powerful ways
I am with you, yes am I saved.

Iscariot

Come, the black robed piper said,
come and taste the victory bled
upon the cross of Him who knew
unto the winds the wings that flew,
up to the Lord of all that is
His Son whose life was worth a kiss,
to the cheek that turned in vain
who would seek eternal shame
not knowing of the price of sin
the death of life from grace given
to all who make their choices clear
for eternity, seek the price to bear—

Upon the soul the silver fell

No need for death in living hell

A very little part of him

A piece of us in his own sin.

The Prince

When I whisper a prayer
on high lifting dawn
my soul is laid down
before a crown of low thorns,

I whisper it full
on the reach of the day,
as light rains down
the faithful will pray,

On the last breath of dusk
we might hope to see
the long hands of darkness
wrap their palms around me,

To remind of a promise
once that was given,
the palms they were pierced
see the nails that were driven,

Deep through the heart
of One who so loved,
I worship you Lord,
Prince of the Doves.

they haunt

I see these things
and they haunt my day,
I see all these things
and I know whom to pray,

the price of one borne
in the mind of the eye
the call will be made
as He makes one to die,

for such is the life
of those who would see
in a mind
in an eye
am I waiting and free,

the Lord will He lift
that which haunts
all my days
and make it the vision
that calls as He saves,

and brings down an age
to its low weary knee
even though cost
finds its toll;
Is that free?

ashes

Scatter my ashes
one long breathless day
and shatter my cares,
small debt to repay,
I am born and I die
on the winds
as they lay
my essence of body
to red bloody clay,
where it mixes
with the fill
of babes to be born,
where it meets
a new form...
By birth is the dawn,
of soldiers anew
who will march
on the morn,
in long-winded evening
they succumb to the call,
such breath that will take
my ashes away,
on a wind that knows only
the short length of day.

His crumbs

May I sit at the back
of your church,
tall people,
with the mice
and the crumbs of a Word,
reach as it would, to
the small ones and me;
could we see past
skyscrapers
worn atop the heads
of those who know much;
may I creep
could I squeak
a little word or two
of my own,
that the Lord might like
to hear?
Listen as He does
for the voices of the
small ones,
down at the back
with the mice
and His crumbs.

the one of lots

I like this game
a little, lot
it thrills myself
to seek the plot
of mighty force
come float around
of lengthy course
in type rebound
upon my willing
illness less
that bastes my soul
in restlessness
Invisibility
takes its toll
I am no man
who'd be so bold
to play the tune
of trading free;
the haute-bazaar
of destiny,
it's there to soothe
my bloodied pride
to salve the scars;
I'd sooner hide
my garments from
this little game,
the one of lots,
the one of shame.

Sour tongue

Damn you, man of words,
your head besieged
by a restless countenance
that would tear your limb
from limb
and lay them on the ground
in a shape
like a cross;
your value, in disparate parts,
such agony
in your own forfeiture
to express by a sour tongue
the hope that burns
within your sweet heart.

Worms

I walk this land,

strange as it seems

to me,

a land of lives

bound to the soil

from whence they came,

and not a word

in sight,

come the time

of gentle return,

to the worms

and the ways

of the earth.

as foam

I am a stranger
in a strange land,
my footsteps light
across the drifts of time,
my face turned
now and again
to the crash of lives
against an unrelenting shore;
as foam,
strewn from the mouth
of unforgiveness.

where pilgrims seek

Of gardens found
on reaching lands
between the clouds
of gentle hands,
that made the
highest whited peak
of snow and hue
as pilgrims seek;
such solace as
a place may give
to fleeting times
abject to live,
in splendid lonely
parting ways
in truth alone
no debt repaid;
now seek you
all that is not there
on lonely peaks
no voice to hear,
these gardens of the herbs
that save
the bitter kind
of shallow grave.

Hounds

I hate that which
is rarely said,
the ticking clock
of temporal dread:

of age and wear
beyond the point
of listless life
and rotting wood,

of days of haze
in memories bound
by shackles set
in shillings, pounds,

and pretty little
consciousness
that flies up with
my loneliness,

to meet the Father
merry-found
is my illusion,
the faithful hound.

The Net

I will not ride
an invisible horse
in the race to a
death I cannot doubt.

What sin is it
to doubt the
mute intonations
of lips that move
silently in the
night of my soul?

What sense can be
made of a place
of dreams that
would leave their
master
to struggle against
the net
he cast for others,
but not for himself,
on his invisible steed?

The Word

Pray come the time
of eventide glow
pray come the light
to those laid below.
By life and its burden
of he who would share,
by death of due hope
of her who dared care.

And laid their lives down
'fore an altar of air
and laid all they could
before that which was bare.
Found naked and scorned
upon wood that was raised
found He who was born
that His Father be praised.

Before darkness fell twice
on that long aged day
as light fled the scene
of a final breath prayed.
That poured from the man
who dwelt in our world
and said "it is done"
so became He the Word.

And praise be to Him
on His altar of air
and gone be the sin
of those who would care.
For they who forgive
be they in turn given
for that which they give
and so are forgiven.

I hear the call

I seek the illusion
I have the delusion
of my age
the words of blue
dance
across the page,
of living love
and living free
I hear the call
of humility.

Beauty Seeks

Beauty seeks me
in all grace
it is my way
the gentle lace,
that covers the face
of stillness born
upon the breath
of early dawn.

Of Him whose light
is pure and clean
of Him whose Son
in you believe,
the gentle way
of delicate lace,
the righteous way
of beautiful face.

A Sinner Born

A sinner born
a sinner be
who knows to walk
upon the knee,
a cross
a hill
I seek for thee,
lo my name
is poverty.

plain days

I delight in the simple days
of my Father,
found in those tasks
and in the doing of such things
as would fill my life with clutter;

to become as one with His wish
that my time be bound
by the cords of loving service,
and in the plainest of days would I find
the truth of His teaching ways.

The nowhere land

the nowhere man says to his Lord,
"come take me from this place,"
the nowhere land
where he kneels
'fore the idols of his faith,

he thought he fought from time begun
a good and spirited fight;
the Lord he saw
the bloodied sword
and made to set it right,

the man he can from lonely sands
look out across the plains,
the nowhere land
set in his heart
the source of all his pain.

just He and me

He took me on
that gentle knee
I said to Him
"Lord let me be,
I cannot do this thing you ask
I'm not perfected for the task,"
His voice returned on evening breeze
it called His Son;
yet more believe,
and left me still upon that knee,
with all that is;
just He and me.

Little Dove

Come, be thee like the little dove
of white and feather
and Lord above,

except thy beak is made of tin
long and sharp
to reach within,

the hearts of those thou doth not like
so where is Christ
and would He white,

the feather from the little dove
of spite and hither,
so little love.

Of Tinnitus

Song of little hell, you dance around my ears
a waltzing thing of smelling breath,
your hold
the touch of living fear;
so trapped within your nightly sheets
a day that knows no rest,
I cannot see beyond the bed
in time no sure release;

I am the one who bought this on,
I am the one who sinned,
and in this highest ringing time
I lay my broken body down;
to rest among the shrieking days,
the noise of little hell
a very modest part of that
in payment came my chiming bells.

Free

Oh please Dear Lord
homeward bound
the steps, the rain
a trodden ground,
a path of many
sleeping years
a path of glory
a way of tears,
that flowed before
the morning light
it was in darkness;
the firefly
did light the way
before the dawn
a spirit found;
the light adorns,
a coming of
our chosen King
the crown of thorns
a chorus rings,
and tells us of
our new birthright,
the steps that cried
with all our might,
oh find me Lord
begotten one,
oh please dear Lord
lift up the sun
and light my way
through all these tears,
your cross my Lord
my sin to bear—
upon your simple
human form
and from my back
the burden borne,
on that day
of Calvary,
Yes my Lord;
I am set free.

About the Author

Patrick McLuskie is an ex-military airline pilot working from and living in Christchurch, New Zealand. He is married to Melissa and they have two adult children, Amelia and William.

Patrick was raised in Upper Hutt, in New Zealand's North Island and attended a Catholic boys' high school. On leaving home he joined the Royal New Zealand Air Force while also completing a Bachelor of Science degree. His military flying included: transporting troops, conducting search and rescue operations, medical evacuations, and the training of entry level pilots on a light jet trainer. Pursuing a commercial flying career he has flown both regional and long haul operations on a variety of aircraft.

After leaving home, Patrick became secular in outlook although he always maintained a sense of a Creator. After joining the airline industry he began to search for God again and became interested in Eastern spiritualties, including Reiki as a healing system as well as reading the Urantia Book for a time.

A family discussion triggered a return to look at the underpinnings of Christianity, this time from a more mature and analytical perspective. To his discomfort, he found the Bible to be sound, logical, and historical. The following years were spent rediscovering his faith in Jesus and eventually settling into a Christian life, after much internal upheaval. He was grounded in the Biblical preaching of the Rev. Philip Lyes and read many of the works of Josh McDowell, Philip Yancey, and Lee Strobel. Most of his poetry was written in a turbulent period of journeying into Christian faith.

All the while, the rest of life was also unfolding; marriage, mortgages, renovations, children, work displacement through redundancy, and Christchurch's major earthquakes were also tracking along with the spiritual journey. His poetry is both experience and observation.

Patrick has a passion for the mountains and has walked many of New Zealand's Great Walks with his family and camera. He also enjoys that great New Zealand institution, the flat white coffee, and the odd craft beer as well.

It is satisfying for Patrick to look back at the "stuff of life" and forward to the publication of this book and any future writing. Patrick and Melissa attended St Augustine's Anglican Church for many years and have more recently attended Grace Vineyard Church in Christchurch. They have a heart for Uganda alongside their dear friends and charitable interests there.

www.ingramcontent.com/pod-product-compliance
Lightning Source LLC
Chambersburg PA
CBHW050803160426
43192CB00010B/1621